THE FIGHT
FOR TOM COD

THE FIGHT FOR TOM COD

Newfoundland in the
American Revolution

GEOFF BENTON

Epigraph Books
Rhinebeck, New York

The Fight for Tom Cod: Newfoundland in the American Revolution © 2020 by Geoff Benton

All rights reserved. No part of this work may be used or reproduced in any manner without the consent of the author except in critical articles or reviews. Contact the publisher for information.

ISBN 978-1-951937-22-5

Library of Congress Control Number 2020903572

Book design by Colin Rolfe

Epigraph Books
22 East Market Street, Suite 304
Rhinebeck, NY 12572
(845) 876-4861
epigraphps.com

*This book is dedicated to my grandmother,
Mary Houlihan Benton.*

CONTENTS

Introduction ix
Chapter One: The Administration of Newfoundland by Great Britain 1
Chapter Two: Economic Entanglement with the American Colonies 11
Chapter Three: Men at War 26
Chapter Four: The War at Sea 33
Chapter Five: The French Join the Fight 39
Chapter Six: The War of Words 49
Epilogue 59
Bibliography 63
Index 72
Acknowledgments 76
About the Author 77

INTRODUCTION

Newfoundland was often the first sight of North America for travelers coming from Europe and the last vision of the New World for those heading back to the old. The island is stuck in the unforgiving North Atlantic like a fortress surrounded by the cold, black water of the Atlantic. For centuries, European powers including the Dutch, the Portuguese, the Basque, and the English and the French in particular, had warred over her storm-battered shores. In 1680 the English Board of Trade had declared "Newfoundland will always belong to the strongest sea power" (Rusted 2011, 11). In the last quarter of the eighteenth century a new power was going to take its turn at shaping Newfoundland, the fledgling United States of America.

Though the American Revolution would not significantly change the governance of Newfoundland, the war would affect the island in almost every other way possible. It hastened the peopling of the island, changed the way life was lived on the island, and helped to create a Newfoundland identity.

How then does a historian of the American Revolution come to study Newfoundland? My grandmother was born in Fox Harbour, Placentia Bay as she liked to say, "on her grandmother's bed." The Avalon Peninsula is still filled with aunts and cousins that, thanks to social media, I am able to keep in touch with. Visiting as a child and teenager, I was shown the fishing village she grew up in and told about my great-great grandfather who was lost when the schooner, *Annie Healy* sank in the August Gale of 1927. I was taken to Castle Hill in Placentia and Signal Hill in St. John's. I saw the Signal Hill Tattoo with its cannons and muskets blazing. And I left, in my youthful ignorance, without a true understanding of what these places meant but with a sense of pride to be at all related to the people of Newfoundland.

In the fullness of time I completed my undergraduate work in history and biology and found that the American Revolution was where I would like to focus my efforts. After a short break from school to work construction, I finished a master's degree in American History. A little less than a decade later I found myself the curator at the historic home of one of America's founders.

Then my grandmother passed away.

After all the sympathy, the kind words, and the funeral I still found myself missing her singing, her dough balls and fish cakes, and her tales of "home." Home, to her, was always Newfoundland, even though she lived in her small house in upstate New York far longer than she did on the island. Her stories of taking boats to the next harbor, of having her leg sewn up by some guy who could sew when she had hit it with an ax trying to split wood, and of not winning the spelling bee at the school where her father was the principal were the soundtrack of my childhood. "I'se da B'y" was my lullaby.

I tried burying myself in work and research both on the job and off. My wife was pregnant with our second child, a son, and I had to be strong for them. As an aside, we named him James after my father and great-grandfather James Houlihan—the latter, the aforementioned principal of Fox Harbour's little school. I whispered this to her in the hospital as we were losing her so that she would know before she was gone. I was looking at correspondence related to the end of the American Revolution at work and reading about Captain James Cook at home. One word kept coming up in both lines of research: Newfoundland.

Then I found this quote that illustrates the importance of Newfoundland to the Revolution by Robert R. Livingston, American Secretary for Foreign Affairs, in a letter to Benjamin Franklin. "I am more and more convinced that every means in your power must be used to secure the Fisheries—They are essential to some states and we cannot but hate the Nation that keeps us from using this common favor of Providence—It was one of the direct objects for carrying on the war" (Livingston, To Benjamin Franklin from Robert R. Livingston, 6 January 1783). But wait, that's not taxation without representation, overpriced tea, liberty, or any of the other myriad of reasons that are typically associated with the beginning of the Revolutionary War. That's fish. Cod fish started the war?

Within a month I had written a short blog post about the importance of the cod fishery to the peace negotiations that ended the war, but my interest was still piqued. Thanks to online shopping, books began to flood my mailbox, since finding histories of Newfoundland at local book stores and libraries proved unsurprisingly difficult. I found myself amazed at the connections I had never known about. I found that the places I had visited as a child played important roles in the war and how the people of Newfoundland stood apart from everyone during the American Revolution. They were too independent to be a true colony yet not radical enough to join the rebellion.

In this book I've sought to connect the wide-ranging effects of the American Revolution on Newfoundland and the effects of Newfoundland on the Revolution—in one convenient place. Many histories, both historic and modern, make mention of the connection of the island to the war, but hopefully, this is the first one to draw all those connections together.

Academically, I hope that by assembling this work in one place I provide a new way to look at the world war aspects of the American Revolution—particularly, how its effects were felt far beyond the original thirteen states. Personally, I hope this book makes my Newfoundland relatives and ancestors proud. For me, writing this

Introduction

has been cathartic—making me feel connected to my Grandmother again in some small way. And it has allowed me to travel back in time to when I stood on Signal Hill looking down at St. John's spread before me, feeling the salt-tinged wind as it blew against me and wondering what it must have been like to sail a schooner or a sloop through the Narrows and into the harbor.

A note on usage in this book. When I refer to *America*, *the Americas* or the *American colonies*, I am referring to the thirteen colonies that signed the Declaration of Independence and became the first version of the United States of America.

So please read on and enjoy.

Chapter 1

THE ADMINISTRATION OF NEWFOUNDLAND BY GREAT BRITAIN

The place: Utrecht, the Netherlands. The year: 1713. More than half a century and an ocean away but the most logical time and place to start a book about Newfoundland during the American Revolution.

Specifically, the Treaty of Utrecht of 1713 that ended the war of Spanish Succession—the latest in a long series of European wars that cost many lives and changed very little. This particular war was fought by France, Spain, Great Britain, Portugal, Sardinia, the Holy Roman Empire, Prussia, Savoy, Denmark, Hungary, several German principalities, and the Netherlands over whether or not a French prince could become King of Spain following the death of Charles II, who died without a Spanish successor. In the end, after more than a decade of fighting the French prince, Philip was allowed to take the throne of Spain as long as he gave up his claim to the crown of France. Four hundred thousand men were killed in battle while the total loss of life in the war amounted to more than 1.2 million people.

According to the treaty, the entire island of Newfoundland was declared an English territory. The French would have to abandon their main base at Plaisance, which became Placentia under the English, and would not be allowed to fortify any other part of the island. French settlers would be moved off the island. In a small concession to the French, they were allowed to continue fishing the banks of Newfoundland and were allowed to dry them on a certain area of the island. This area ran from Point Riche to Cape Bonavista on the northern coast of the island and became known as "The French Shore." The French were not to spend any more time in Newfoundland waters than was absolutely necessary (Suthern 2000, 125).

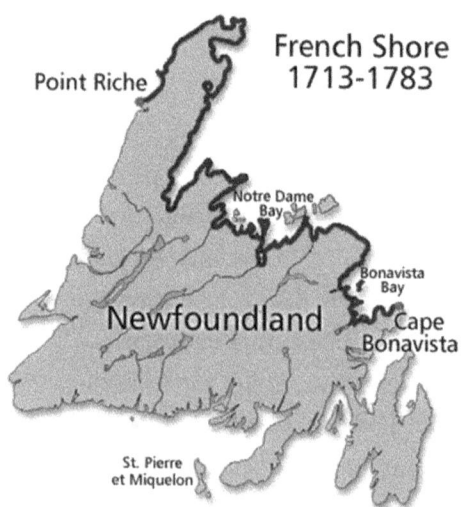

Figure 1. The French Shore in Newfoundland from 1713 to 1783. Courtesy of Newfoundland and Labrador Heritage (Hiller 2001).

Of course, this did not finalize possession of the island for the European powers. In 1754 a twenty-two-year-old Virginian by the name of George Washington, leading a small group of Virginia militiamen and Native Americans, ambushed a French army patrol in the Ohio country and sparked the French and Indian War, also known as the Seven Years' War in much of the rest of the world. Newfoundland once again became a battleground.

On June 27, 1762 a French Army under the command of the Comte d'Haussonville was able to force the English garrison defending St. John's to surrender. They occupied the defensive positions around the town and prepared for the inevitable counterattack, which came on September 15, 1762.

A combined force of British regular army soldiers and militia drawn from the American colonies under the command of William Amherst surprised the 295 French defenders on Signal Hill. After a brief fire-fight, the British took the hill. The rest of the French defenders of St. John's retreated into Fort William. The British navy, ever ready to perform a miracle, raised cannons up the steep sides of Signal Hill using rope and manpower. Once on top of the hill the cannons could threaten the rest of St. John's. They bombarded the fort for three days from this advantageous position. In the end, fifteen hundred French soldiers had no choice but to surrender. The Battle of Signal Hill has the distinction of being the last military action of the war in North America (Janzen 2013, 150).

The Treaty of Paris signed the following year, 1763, once

again changed the fishing industry off Newfoundland. The French lost all their Canadian colonies but did retain the right to fish on the Newfoundland banks. In order to have a place to dry and salt their fish to prepare it for transportation they were allowed to use the French Shore granted to them by the Treaty of Utrecht. In addition, they were given possession of two small islands off the south coast of Newfoundland, Saint Pierre and Miquelon.

Coincidentally, the French arrived at St. Pierre and Miquelon to take possession of the islands on the same day that Captain James Cook arrived to do his hydrographic survey of the islands. Cook spent most of the 1760s charting the coast of Newfoundland in such detail that the charts he created would not be superseded for hundreds of years. Obviously, the Navy put a high degree of value on this work, so spent several days making excuses as to why the French could not take possession of the islands yet in order to give Cook the time he needed to complete his surveys (Suthern 2000, 131).

English fishermen would continue to use the southeastern part of Newfoundland, the Avalon Peninsula, as they had for generations. Every spring, ships would arrive in the harbors and ports of the island, loaded with men to fish and women and children to handle the salting, drying, and packing jobs on shore. Some of the ships' paying passengers intended to continue on to other colonies. Some of them never left Newfoundland and helped to swell the population (Thompson 1961, 14). They would join the full-time residents of the island, merchants, artisans, servants, and some fishermen who hunkered down on the island every winter. At the end of the season most fishermen would return to their home ports in England, but some would stay, having decided to take the freedom that the island offered or perhaps having married a woman on Newfoundland. Slowly, the full-time population of the island grew (Kerr 1941, 56).

West Country merchant men, who had a near monopoly on the fishing trade until the 1770s, were responsible for sending the majority of men to Newfoundland to fish. Merchants, particularly from Liverpool, funded the yearly fishing trips and reaped the majority of the profits. At times the fishermen were simply referred to as "Liverpool men." For example, Cotton Tufts, a cousin to John Adams, in a letter to his cousin recommended sending privateers to Newfoundland to do damage "among the Liverpool Men" (Tufts 1776). While the merchants would have preferred that the fishermen they hired be English, beginning around 1670 a large portion of the men who went fishing were Irish. Often times, the men left to perform the winter duties were Irish. This led to a rapidly increasing proportion of Irish amongst the island's full-time population. By 1753 all the communities of the Avalon Peninsula had Irish majorities. By the time the American Revolution broke out it's likely that up to half of the island's full-time population was Irish (Campey 2016, 55).

Though women came with the fishing fleet every spring, the vast majority of the population remained male. During his 1766 visit to the island, Joseph Banks attended a formal ball thrown by the navy. The need to find women to match the men in attendance for dancing was so great that he noted a washerwoman and her sister were in attendance at the ball by formal invitation (Banks 1971, 146).

Women who came to the island were putting themselves at risk. In addition to the hardships of the Atlantic crossing and harsh conditions on the island, they also faced a population of men who lived on the edge of civilization and who sometimes crossed the edge into barbarity. In 1751 three soldiers from the St. John's garrison attacked and raped Elizabeth Melville, the seventeen-year-old servant of Ann Moore, in a strawberry patch near the town. Only one of the soldiers was found guilty of the crime (O'Neil 2003, 487).

On the French Shore, French fishermen found that, in their absence, many English fishermen had moved into their territory. They had either taken over or destroyed French houses, flakes, and vessels left on the shore. This led to a diplomatic dispute. The French argued the Treaty of Utrecht gave them exclusive rights to that shore, that they alone could inhabit it. The English argued the right was concurrent, that they had as much right to use the north coast of the island as the French. This dispute was never soundly settled because of the outbreak of the American Revolution.

For the British, Newfoundland was never meant to be a true colony. It was thought it might be made a colony in 1765, but a new Board of Trade in 1766 recommended the antisettlement policies be much more strongly enforced (Matthews 1988). English Statesman William Knox put the English idea of Newfoundland best in a 1793 testimony to the House of Commons when he called it "a great English ship moored near the fishing banks during the season" (Webb 2015, 112). Occasionally, efforts were made to push out people who had settled permanently on the island. English racism was on full display here as Irish Catholics were far more likely to be evicted from the island than their English protestant counterparts (Campey 2016). The simple fact is the antisettlement fight in Newfoundland was lost by the time of the English Civil War, when more and more fishermen began staying on the island to avoid the fighting at home in England (Cadigan 1995, 27).

Administration of Newfoundland was officially in the hands of whichever admiral or commodore was in command of the Newfoundland Squadron. This was an improvement from the times past when the first fishing captain to reach the island was in charge for the season. The admiral was usually headquartered at St. John's. The deputy commander of the fleet was usually headquartered at Placentia. The biggest problem with this system is that it left the island ungoverned for about six months out of the year because the Admiral sailed in with the fleet sometime in the spring and sailed out again at the end of the fishing season, usually around October.

This led to Newfoundland and St. John's getting a

deservedly rough reputation. Joseph Banks, the famous British naturalist, visited St. John's a few times during his excursions to Canada. He called St. John's "the Most Disagreeable Town I ever met with" (Banks 1971, 146). Drinking was a main pastime. In 1775 the city had a population of about fifteen hundred people but imported 250,000 gallons of rum. That's more than 160 gallons of rum per person in the city. Obviously, at least some of this rum went out on fishing vessels or was traded to outports, but much of it went to supply the eighty licensed public houses in the city. There were stories of drunken children roaming the streets of the city (O'Neil 2003, 166). Even more scandalous, it was almost common for men and women to live together outside of wedlock. Outside of St. John's, it was quite common for people not to keep the Sabbath, being more involved in the business of staying alive. In short it was said that for six months of the year the people of Newfoundland were left to "all kinds of wickedness and debauchery" (Kerr 1941, 61).

That is not to say that this reputation for debauchery was unearned. Living in a dangerous land and working in one of the most dangerous professions in the world could wear on anyone. A British Parliamentary Commission assigned to look at the Newfoundland fishery found that at least one thousand men died per year due to wrecks and foundering in bad weather (T. Williams 2009, 208). The men and women who stayed on the island year-round deserved every bit of recreation they got because there was a very real possibility that they might not survive the next season.

Newfoundland was not completely lawless, though. There were jails where people could be held by the sheriff or constables. There were coroners and even a grand jury that could decide to hold the accused for a trial (Bannister 1998, "Convict Transport and the Colonial State in Newfoundland, 1789"). Usually they were held until the governor returned for the year and could hold court. It was said that the navy settled any dispute that could not be settled with a fist fight (T. Williams 2009, 213). In 1777 Lawrence Hallohan and Lawrence Dalton both appeared before the admiral/royal governor on the charge of forgery. Both were sentenced to be hanged for their crimes (O'Neil 2003, 387). The other very common punishment in Newfoundland was banishment or transportation. This meant that, after being found guilty, the criminal was put on a ship headed back to England or Ireland or sometimes to the American colonies and forbidden from ever returning to Newfoundland on pain of death.

There are also examples of the Newfoundland justice system as being as unfair as those found throughout Western countries in the eighteenth century. Specifically, it was unfair to the poor. In 1777 Richard Power was accused of hitting John Cahill with a stone and killing him. He was found not guilty of the crime but still kept in jail because he could not pay his court fees (O'Neil 2003, 387).

To be a fisherman or a colonist one had to have a little streak of rebellion in him. For much of Newfoundland's history, the very act of staying on the island, if not explicitly illegal, was officially discouraged. Of course, those people who were willing to bend that law were willing to bend other laws, including those that tied them to England economically.

Chapter 2

ECONOMIC ENTANGLEMENT WITH THE AMERICAN COLONIES

Over the course of the eighteenth century the economy of Newfoundland had become an important part of the complex network of trade that linked the colonies of the western hemisphere. This involved Newfoundland in the slave economy that funded the European conquest of the Western Hemisphere. It also represented a threat to the British colonial system, as Newfoundland and the American colonies were cutting England out as middleman by trading directly with each other.

The cod caught off Newfoundland had two main destinations. The best quality fish was bound for Spain and Portugal. Fishermen could "look upon every cod pulled up into the vessel as a certain quantity silver ore which required only carrying to Spain to be coined into pieces of eight" (B. Franklin 1729). This continued throughout the century. By 1769 the Newfoundland fishery was valued at: at least £600,000. Dried cod was the fourth most valuable commodity exported from the colonies prior to the American Revolution. (Magra 2007, 1). This was not only for the high quality fish sold in Europe but for the lower quality fish that would be used for a much more insidious purpose.

Figure 2; Cod Fish, Courtesy of the New York Public Library

For all the fighting the English and French did over the American and Canadian colonies, none of them ever turned a profit. The money crop of the colonial era was sugar. It could only be grown in a small area and was incredibly labor intensive, but for the owners of sugar plantations it was worth a fortune. These plantations were primarily located in the Caribbean on islands like Barbados, Saint-Domingue, and Jamaica. Brazil and Surname were also major producers of sugar on mainland South America. Sugar was so valuable that plantation owners did not want to turn any of the arable land in the Caribbean over to food production when it could be used to grow more sugar cane.

This meant that that most of the food used to feed not

Economic Entanglement with the American Colonies

only the resident plantation owners, but also the thousands upon thousands of enslaved people that labored on the plantations, had to be imported from elsewhere. It is believed that, during the four-hundred-year period European powers used enslaved Africans for labor on their sugar plantations, more than ten million enslaved people were brought to the Caribbean, many of whom would die from disease or mistreatment.

Herein lay the value of the other colonies. Going back well into the seventeenth century, when the Dutch were still a true power in the Atlantic world they would transport wheat from their colony of New Netherland (which became New York when they lost it to the English in 1664) to their territories in the Caribbean to feed the enslaved people. Wheat could be sent ground into flour to be cooked there or baked into hard tack that could be stored for months, or even years, without becoming inedible.

But man cannot live on carbohydrates alone. Protein is needed to keep muscles going. For the English this meant bringing the lower quality cod, the refuse cod, from Newfoundland to the sugar colonies. Once dried, cod is nutritionally up to 80 percent protein (Magra 2006, 102). In the English model, ideally, the fish would be brought back to England or Ireland before being sent to the Caribbean. This way they could collect both import and export duties on the fish, and the crown got its cut of the trade. Of course there were some ship owners who at the end of the fishing season would brave the Atlantic hurricane season, or more likely order their crews to brave the

Atlantic hurricane season, and bring the fish directly to the sugar colonies so that they could undercut the more legally delivered fish. This seems to have been rare though (Janzen, "The Revolution as Opportunity" 2001).

The much more common method for cutting the English crown out of the trade developed between Newfoundlanders and New Englanders. New Englanders frequently fished the Grand Banks and put in to Newfoundland ports and harbors to dry their catch. Soon, some of the more industrious New Englanders and some New Yorkers realized they could turn a good profit bringing wheat, bread, vegetables, and even livestock from their home ports and trading them for fish (Matthews 1988, 116). They would then transport the fish to the sugar colonies and return with sugar and molasses. By the 1740s New England was doing as much trade with the Caribbean as it was with England (Kurlansky 1998, 94). Some of the sugar and molasses was sold in their home ports but some would be saved and sold to the Newfoundlanders, although the molasses could fetch a higher price once it had been distilled into rum.

This trade was increasingly important for the Newfoundlanders, particularly at the end of the fishing season for those who would remain on the island for the winter. By the middle of the eighteenth century the West Country merchants that controlled the fishery accepted the illicit trade because they recognized they could not provide the quantity of food that the Americans did for anywhere near the same price (Newfoundland Historical

Society 2008, 59). The food helped to get them through the winter. By 1767 there were less than fifteen hundred acres of land under active cultivation in Newfoundland, as most people saw Newfoundland as a place of business and not a place to settle (Kerr 1941, 57). This was not nearly enough to feed even the reduced population that wintered-over on the island. It also provided the basis for the provisions for the following year's fishing fleet, which meant that ships coming in the spring could carry more people and less food on the western leg of the trip.

Shortly before the American Revolution broke out, two things happened that forever changed the way this relationship worked. On March 25, 1774 the British Parliament passed the Boston Port Act, which completely closed the port of Boston—no ships in or out until the citizens of Boston repaid in full the value of the tea dumped in the harbor on December 16, 1773. The Boston Tea Party, as it was known, was protest against the Tea Act of 1773 that gave the East India Company a monopoly to sell tea in the colonies. Not only could the company then cut colonial tea merchants out of the market, but the act also tacked a small tax onto each pound of tea. Another tax to be paid by the colonists.

The Boston Port Act was the first of four acts known in America as the Coercive Acts. They were intended to isolate the city of Boston and the colony of Massachusetts from the rest of the colonies and stamp out the revolutionary spirit growing there. Unfortunately for the British, the acts had the complete opposite effect in that they rallied other colonies to the cause of Boston and Massachusetts. Foodstuffs and other supplies poured in from other colonies, and they ended up more unified than they ever had been in the past.

Figure 3. The Boston Tea Party. Courtesy of the Library of Congress

The Boston Port Act also had the unintended side effect of causing near-starvation conditions in Newfoundland in the spring of 1775. Because the port of Boston was closed in 1774 many of the ships that normally would have sailed to Newfoundland loaded with food and other provisions never left port. When the fishing fleet arrived in the spring loaded not only with sailors, but also with passengers and people who were destined to work the shore-bound side of the trade, the salting and drying the fish on the flakes—they found the food supplies on the island already stretched to the limit, and there was simply not enough food to feed the influx of new people (Matthews 1988). Ships were dispatched to Quebec and

Economic Entanglement with the American Colonies

back to England, Ireland, and Scotland for food, but this took time and cut sharply into the profits of the fishing season. A letter dated June 12 in the *New York Journal* states: "The necessities of the people here for bread, are increasing daily; the laborers and fishermen have some time been at short allowance, and I am informed that many families have not any to eat" (Extract of a letter from Newfoundland dated June 12, 1775). Evidence becomes scarce as you move away from St. John's, but there are stories of people in outports starving to death during this period. One writer from Conception Bay said "There is a raging famine, None can express the heart felt woe of women and children mourning for want of food" (Major 2002, 159). As a result of the food shortage, the people of Newfoundland began to farm in greater numbers than they had previously. Hundreds of acres were burned to clear them of trees and make them suitable for farming, but harvesting crops planted then was months in the future (Kerr 1941, 72–73).

This lack of vessels from the Americas became the new normal. In 1774, even with Boston closed, 175 American vessels had arrived to trade in Newfoundland. This represented a quantity of goods barely enough to get the resident population of Newfoundland through the winter and not enough to support the spring fishing. In 1775 the number of American trading ships dropped to sixty-six. In 1776 it dropped even further to just three (Janzen 2013).

On April 19, 1775 a column of about seven

hundred British soldiers marched out of Boston into the Massachusetts countryside. Their mission was to seize cannons and other weapons stored in a little town called Concord a few miles away by the patriots' shadow government. To do so they had to march through another small town called Lexington. There they were greeted by about eighty militia men formed in ranks on the village green. A shot was fired, though history will never know by whom, that led to a general musket fire. Several of the militia men were killed and the rest dispersed.

The British soldiers marched on to Concord where they were met by even more militiamen. After a tense standoff, the two sides began firing at each other. The British suddenly found themselves vastly outnumbered. They fought a running battle all the way back to the outskirts of Boston that left more than two hundred British soldiers wounded or dead. Boston was soon surrounded by an army of militiamen, not only from Massachusetts but also from the surrounding colonies. The army may have swelled to as many as thirty thousand men. Suddenly, Britain found itself at war with its own colonies.

Among the first acts of the Continental Congress after the war began was to ban the export of food to Newfoundland. On June 7, 1775 John Adams, a Continental Congress delegate from Massachusetts, wrote to Isaac Smith Sr., a relative of Adams's wife and a loyalist recently sailed for England, "that not a pound of flour, or bread, or meat goes from any of these colonies to supply that fishery" (Adams 1775). William Hooper, a Continental Congress delegate from North Carolina, called it "a just retaliation for restraining the American fishery" (Letters of Delegates to Congress 1774-1789 1976, 400).

Smuggling reportedly became a problem for nascent government to control. Less than two months later at the end of July, James Warren, President of the Massachusetts Provincial Congress, wrote to Adams; "I am well informed that Newfoundland is supplied with provisions from New York." (Warren, To John Adams from James Warren, 31 July 1775 1775) There was also some pushback from the Massachusetts delegates who did not want to ban the trade because of the debts owed to them by the Newfoundlanders (Letters of Delegates to Congress 1774-1789 1976, 397). Nonetheless, the number of American ships continued to drop, as previously shown. Ship owners and captains quickly became afraid to risk their ships, crews, and freedom to the British navy for the profits a trading trip to Newfoundland could provide. Many of these ships and crews soon found themselves otherwise employed as privateers as the war progressed.

Just as Newfoundland was recovering from the starvation of the early part of the 1775 fishing season, another disaster struck. On September 5, perhaps dawn was red that morning and distant hills appeared near. Perhaps the gulls flew high and the goats came home—but soon the sea began to look angry. Then, suddenly one of the fiercest hurricanes in memory hit the island. Placentia Bay, Trinity Bay, Conception Bay, and St. John's were all devastated. Ships and boats trying to squeeze in a few more days of fishing were lost. Seas up to thirty-feet high swept ashore and took thousands of pounds of drying cod, buildings and people back out to sea with them. Just a few days later another hurricane of nearly equal force hit the island. Up to four thousand people died. Hundreds of bodies were caught in nets over the next several days and bones washed ashore for years to come. The stench of dead people and rotting cod was nearly overwhelming as one approached the island (T. Williams 2009, 227, 235). Joseph Palmer, a brigadier general in the Massachusetts militia, wrote to John Adams in December of that year to tell the story of a British lieutenant who had supposedly been sent to Newfoundland to recruit troops for the British army then under siege in Boston. He had been successful in getting troops but upon seeing the destruction wrought by the storm thought that "God almighty was against 'em" and immediately gave up his commission and refused to take part in the war against the colonies (Palmer 1775). While the story is likely untrue in its particulars, it is quite clear that the destructive force that hit Newfoundland was unlike anything most had seen before. Palmer's mysterious British lieutenant was not the only one to see the hurricane as a symbol of God's favor for the rebelling colonies. James Warren wrote to John Adams in December of 1775 to say, "The Great Loss at Newfoundland &c I think may be considered as An Interposition of Providence in our favor" (Warren, "To John Adams from James Warren, 3 December 1775"

Economic Entanglement with the American Colonies

1775). For the Newfoundlanders it would mean another year of near starvation and deprivation. It was not until 1777 that the West Country merchants who controlled much of the Newfoundland fishery were able to begin sending food and other provisions from the United Kingdom in great enough quantities to keep the people fed (Matthews 1988, 118).

Palliser's Act of 1775 had been passed by the British Parliament in an attempt to, among other things, keep New England fishermen away from Newfoundland. Created by former Governor Admiral Hugh Palliser, the act was designed to encourage the seasonal fishing trade of Newfoundland by incentivizing the return to England and Ireland by the fishermen at the end of the season by withholding part of their pay until they got back to their home port. It also banned colonists from the American colonies from drying their fish on Newfoundland (Webb 2015, 116). So, the act was a double blow to Americans as it cut into their fishery as well as the business of supplying the island.

Figure 4. Hugh Palliser Courtesy of the New York Public Library.

Frederick, Lord North, Great Britain's Prime Minister at the time, also put forth his own act that moved that

Figure 5. Lord North. Courtesy of the Library of Congress.

the American colonies be banned from engaging in the Newfoundland Grand Banks fishery. This was a purely punitive measure taken because of other transgressions the Americans had committed against the crown. He said, "the fishery on the Banks of Newfoundland and the other banks, and all others in America was the undoubted right of Great Britain. Therefore we might dispose of them as we please" (*New York Gazette* 1775). While the limited size of the Newfoundland naval squadron made enforcement challenging, it certainly was enough to take away some of the incentive for New Englanders to sail into northern waters.

The American response to this was less than enthusiastic. In preparing notes to address Parliament, Benjamin Franklin, who represented several colonies in England at the time, wrote, "the fisheries possessed by the French there and on the Banks of Newfoundland, so far as they were more extended then at present , was made by the joint forces of Britain and the colonies, the latter having nearly an equal number of men in the service with the former it follows that the colonies have an equitable and just right to participate in the Advantage of those fisheries" (Franklin 1775). In short, Americans had already fought for the cod fishery. How could England now take away the right they had earned to it? This mirrors something Franklin had written in 1767. "It is reasonable, O ye Americans! that though you fought bravely, in conjunction with us to obtain and secure the fisheries of Newfoundland and Labrador, yet you shall not enjoy a freedom of fishing there in common with other British Subjects or even the freedom allowed by the peace, to our enemies" (Franklin 1767). This piece of satire illustrated how the right to fishery had been earned by the Americans and that limiting their access to it was an abomination of free government.

Many of the New Englanders cut off from the fishery by the British government, unfairly in their perception, would join George Washington's army. Historian Christopher P. Magra once wrote, "The American Revolution cannot be fully understood without coming to terms with the military mobilization of the commercial fishing industry" (Magra 2007, 799). The American Revolution and George Washington's army were saved more than once by a regiment made up of former cod fishermen from Marblehead, Massachusetts.

Following the British abandonment of Boston on March 17, 1776, General George Washington, now in charge of the American Continental Army, gambled that the next target for the British would be New York City, and he moved most of his troops there. He spread his troops out on Long Island and Manhattan Island. The

The Fight for Tom Cod

British arrived in New York harbor on June 29, 1776. This was one of the largest water-borne invasions ever, made up of hundreds of ships and more than thirty thousand soldiers and sailors. Just two months later, on August 27 the British attacked the American positions on Long Island and soon had the Continentals on the run to the western tip of the island. Expecting either the start of a brief siege or a quick battle in the morning, the British went to sleep on August 29 with what was left of the American army trapped between them and the water. They awoke the next morning to find the American army gone. Overnight, the Marblehead fisherman under the command of Colonel John Glover had rowed the majority of the American army away from Long Island to Manhattan. In a stroke of luck for the Americans, a dense fog had shielded them from the eyes of British army scouts as the skilled fishermen rowed, saving the army from almost certain destruction by the invading British under General William Howe. The Revolution would live on for another day.

On Christmas of that same year the Marblehead sailors once again brought the entire army across a body of water. This time it was the Delaware River. In the course of just a few hours the cod fishermen rowed the entire army across the river, making trip after trip, so that in the morning they were ready to attack the hired Hessian soldiers encamped at Trenton. This led to the first major American victory of the war and helped keep the fires of rebellion burning through the cold winter.

Economic Entanglement with the American Colonies

The New England fisherman fought on land and on sea. Hundreds of fishing vessels had gun ports cut in their sides, sails added, and their planking reinforced. They obtained their licenses from either the Continental Congress or their state government and put to sea as privateers to harass British trade and eventually the Newfoundland fishery (Magra 2004, 556).

The New England fishermen often fished the same waters and with the same methods as their Newfoundland cousins. The New England merchants tied Newfoundlandthe island to the colonies with supplies of bread, vegetables, and rum. When this trade was disrupted by the British policies that led to the American Revolution, the New England fishermen rebelled. For Newfoundlanders though, the choice was not that simple.

Chapter 3

MEN AT WAR

The people of Newfoundland faced starvation in 1775. The need to send ships to Canada and to Europe in search of food left many hundreds of men ashore with no employment. Rather than turn to rebellion many Newfoundlanders would choose or be chosen to fight for the British army and navy.

It has been theorized that one of the reasons that Newfoundland did not join the rebellion against the British was that they had no central government to rally behind. In the American colonies there was a body elected by the colonists to assist the royal governor with leading the colony. Their powers varied from colony to colony, but they were always included in the colonial charters that acted as the constitutions for the colonies. As relations with the British government grew worse, it was often these governing bodies that formed the heart of the resistance.

Newfoundland simply did not have anything similar. There was no colonial body for the people to rally behind. There was not even a newspaper printed in

Newfoundland at this time to spread the words of rebellion. The first newspaper printed in Newfoundland was not started until 1807 (O'Neil 2003, 115). Too often, in Newfoundland life was simply about survival.

All this made Newfoundland a prime target for military recruiters when the war began. Two captains of the 42nd Regiment of Foot, then stationed in Quebec, arrived in Newfoundland in early 1775 to recruit for their regiment. They quickly filled their quotas with young, jobless, and hungry Irishmen who had come over to work in the fishing industry. The British army might be brutal and dangerous, but at least it guaranteed food for its soldiers. The fishing industry was also brutal and dangerous but at that time could not guarantee food.

In August of 1775 newly minted American General Richard Montgomery departed Fort Ticonderoga with a group of about twelve hundred soldiers to invade Canada, which at the time mostly meant Quebec. Montgomery had served in the British army for nearly twenty years, fighting in both North America and the Caribbean during the French and Indian War. He resigned from the army and moved to the colony of New York. He married into the Livingston family, one of the richest and most powerful families in the colony, also one of the most anti-British. When the war broke out, his experience as a soldier and his new family connections won him an appointment as a brigadier general and a place as second in command of the planned invasion of Canada. He quickly became the commander of the invasion, though, when the commanding officer, Major General Philip Schuyler, came down with a very convenient case of gout and had to stay home.

It was thought that a show of force would quickly make the residents of Quebec join the Revolution. Having so recently been ceded to Britain by France, many felt the *Quebecois* would love the chance to escape British rule. However, British rule of Quebec had been mostly hands-off, allowing the Quebecois to maintain their own language and religious practice. The inspiration to join the American cause was minimal. Aside from an understrength regiment raised by a distant cousin to Montgomery's family, James Livingston, aid from the Canadians was almost nonexistent.

Montgomery had some early success in his invasion. He laid siege to the fort at St. John's, Quebec. It fell on November 3, 1775 after a relief attempt by General Sir Guy Carleton, commander of British forces in Canada and a veteran of the French and Indian War in Canada, failed to reach the fort. Montreal fell soon thereafter, and only Quebec City remained as a major holdout against the Americans.

Carleton had been preparing for this situation though. In October 1775 one hundred carpenters and other artificers had been transported to the city from Newfoundland to construct defenses and serve as soldiers if the city was attacked. On November 12, Captain Campbell of the 42nd Regiment arrived with forty of his Newfoundland recruits. Another ninety arrived the next day. On

Men at War

December 5, Montgomery, who had recently united his command with that of Benedict Arnold, began a siege of Quebec. Their combined force amounted to about eleven hundred men against the eighteen hundred fighting men inside the walls of Quebec. Thirteen percent of the men behind the walls were Newfoundlanders.

On December 31, 1775 Montgomery and Arnold launched a two-pronged attack on the city in desperate attempt to conquer it before their army dissolved in the winter chill. Montgomery's wing of the attack fell apart when he and several of his officers were killed by a cannon loaded with grapeshot. Arnold's wing also stalled out in the streets of the city. Arnold was wounded and carried off the field but the famous rifleman Daniel Morgan and his men continued to fight on. Captain MacDougal

Figure 6. The Death of General Montgomery. Courtesy of the Library of Congress.

of the 42nd led a group of his Newfoundlanders and Highlanders to flank Morgan. This led to intense hand-to-hand fighting and, eventually, as morning broke Morgan was forced to surrender (Fardy 1995, 4–9).

The remaining American soldiers kept up the siege of the city. Throughout the spring they were reinforced occasionally. The reinforcements never came in great enough numbers to try to take the city again but enough to make the threat of another attack seem very real to Carleton and the other defenders. Carleton ordered the men to sleep in their clothes and on their arms in case an attack should come at night. This was easy for the Newfoundlanders, most of whom had not had a change of clothes in four months. Less easy for them was the postponement of St. Patrick's Day celebrations, which was done specifically to keep the Newfoundlanders from being too drunk to be of service should the Americans attack (Fardy 1995, 11).

The siege of Quebec was finally lifted in May 1776, when the ice on the St. Lawrence River melted enough to allow British reinforcements and provisions through to the city. The Americans lacked the fire power to stop them and began to retreat into New York. The Newfoundlanders were allowed a day to celebrate St. Patrick. When Carleton formed his army on the Plains of Abraham outside the city walls, the Newfoundlanders held the places of honor in the formation. Carleton noted both the soldiers and artificers from Newfoundland in particular in his report on the siege to the British command (Fardy 1995, 25).

The Newfoundland soldiers who had been recruited into the army to fight for Quebec were soon combined with other recruits into a unit known as the Highland Emigrants. This battalion was under the command of Colonel Allan Maclean. Maclean was able to push the British Army to have the Highland Emigrants added to the official army list, making them British soldiers instead of militia. The new Regiment was known as the 84th Regiment of Foot.

On October 23, 1776 parts of the 84th Regiment of Foot took part in one of the most unusual battles of the war, the Battle of Newcastle Jane. The *Newcastle Jane* was a transport ship carrying men of the regiment, as well as uniforms and money to pay the regiment. An American privateer mistook this military transport for a typical merchantman off of Cape Race. Closing to within thirty yards, the Americans received a wicked surprise when the men of the 84th aboard the *Newcastle Jane* opened fire with the six three pound carriage guns, swivel guns and muskets. The ships maneuvered and fired on each other for a full twenty-four hours before the privateer was forced to withdraw because of damage and casualties. The *Newcastle Jane* had only two shots left for her cannon. She was declared the first merchant ship to have defeated an American privateer in the war.

The First Battalion of the 84th Regiment, which would have included the Newfoundland recruits, was used mainly in defending Canada and for occasionally launching raids into the Champlain Valley of New York. Some of the Second Battalion of the 84th Regiment was used to garrison Fort Frederick in Placentia. At the end of the war the 84th Regiment was completely disbanded.

In 1778 two captains of the King's Orange Rangers recruited in Newfoundland. They were not nearly as successful in recruiting troops as British officers had been in 1775. The threat of starvation had been lifted by that time, but more importantly, the war had come home for many Newfoundlanders. They were faced with the much more important task of defending their fisheries and their island. They no longer had time to go off and fight elsewhere.

Chapter 4

THE WAR AT SEA

Newfoundland was always an American target during the Revolutionary War. The Americans needed to hurt the British in whatever way they could. Attacking Newfoundland would of course upset the fishing trade that was, as we have already seen, worth nearly £600,000. In addition, a great deal of Great Britain's power was derived from her nearly invincible reputation upon the seas. Even before the Declaration of Independence was signed in 1776 the Americans had already handed the British army a number of stinging defeats and costly victories, but they had no way to produce a Navy that could in any way rival that of Great Britain. Striking at Newfoundland was a way to sting the British navy, a way to hurt them and perhaps make them change their tactics to allow further stings elsewhere. Most importantly though, it was a way to cost the empire money. Nearly two thousand privateers would be the wasps that stung at the British Empire at sea (Horwood 2011, 118).

Newfoundland had its own squadron of British warships based at St. John's to defend the island and the fishery from attack. In 1775 this squadron consisted of: the *Romney*, a frigate of fifty guns; the *Surprize,* a frigate of twenty-eight guns; two sloops of war; and a few armed cutters and schooners. It was not an overwhelming force by any means and one that would be spread thin to handle what was required of it. Luckily for them, in 1775 there was still a hope in the American colonies that peace with Great Britain—and, more importantly, the economic status quo—could be reestablished.

By 1776 it was apparent that this was not going to happen. The Declaration of Independence meant that the colonies would not be rejoining the empire without a real fight. In 1776 orders began to flow to the fledgling Continental navy, the navies of the individual states, and to privateers. Newfoundland and her fisheries were a target. Over the course of the next two years, American vessels had nearly free rein to destroy the fishery. Among the earliest orders sent by the newly independent United States was to order Commodore Esek Hopkins, commander and chief of the new American navy, to take a squadron of American ships to cruise off Newfoundland (Fowler 1976). He was also ordered to make "prisoners of the fishermen or at least those that will not join us freely" (*Letters of the Delegates of Congress, 1774-1789* 1979, 45). This proved to be a little ambitious as Hopkins had neither the ships, nor the men ready to accomplish this. But the idea was planted, and other ships would soon be sailing for Newfoundland waters.

The first targets were the banks fishing schooners. Not

only were these ships often alone and virtually unprotected, making them easy targets for the privateers but a privateer, could extend its own voyage by raiding the schooners for water, food and naval stores. This is not to say that the American ships did not take Newfoundland vessels for profit as well. On November 14, 1776, Major General Artemas Ward, whom George Washington had left in command of Massachusetts when he departed for New York, reported to Washington that the *Franklin* and the *Hancock* had just arrived in Boston with two prize brigs from Newfoundland. The ships carried a combined 430 quintals of cod, 420 tierces of salmon, and sundry dry goods—for a total value of between £20,000 and £30,000. (Ward 1776).

During the summer of 1776, John Paul Jones, perhaps the most famous American sea captain of the war, operated in the waters off of Newfoundland. He captured sixteen prizes that summer. In the fall he took four ships from the fledgling American navy and again attacked the fishery. Though most of his companion ships had to turn around, Jones was successful on his cruise and returned to Boston in December with three of the seven ships he had taken as prizes and 140 prisoners (Fowler 1976, 97).

American privateers continued scouring the seas for fishermen into 1777. Early in the year the privateer *Rattlesnake* took a brig off Newfoundland (Fitzgerald 1777). Later that year another ship was taken by a Captain Lee which contained dry goods, fish, salt, and 1,000 shirts (Gordon 1777). Perhaps even more humiliating than the constant attacks from the American privateers was the fact that what few British ships were available on the station were forbidden from any spirited pursuit of the privateers because of the scarcity of supplies, like sails and ropes, that could be damaged in such pursuit, making them too valuable to risk (Janzen 2013, 200–201). Even worse was when a ship was lost due to sheer bad luck. In November 1778 the armed sloop *Penguin* was wrecked on the rocks at the south end of Bay Bulls in a storm. Though crew was saved, her commanding officer, Lieutenant Thomas Revelle Shivers, and the entire crew were court-martialed for the loss of the ship. All were found not guilty because of the bad weather and treacherous waters of Newfoundland (The Lords of the Admiralty 1779).

The success that American privateers had in seizing prizes in Newfoundland waters even affected some French fishing vessels. A ship owner, G. Anquetil Brutiere, wrote to Benjamin Franklin, the United States minister to France, on June 7, 1778 asking for compensation. A ship he owned that had been sent to Newfoundland to fish was boarded by the American privateer *Bellona* out of Marblehead. This in itself was not an unusual circumstance. Normally, the fishing captain would simply present the privateer crew with his papers proving who he was, the two crews would exchange news, possibly trade some small goods, and then be on their way. However, this time the *Bellona's* captain put seven English prisoners he had captured from another ship on board Brutiere's ship. The food they consumed shortened the fishing vessel's trip by a full month and cost Brutiere between four thousand and five thousand cod, so he sought compensation (Brutiere 1778).

In the spring of 1777, the American frigates *Hancock* and *Boston* set sail for the Grand Banks. Over the course of the summer they were joined and left by a number of privateers. Together, they burned at least thirty fishing vessels. Then they stumbled upon the British frigate *Fox*, which had twenty-eight guns. The *Hancock* engaged the *Fox* broadside-to-broadside while the *Boston* maneuvered to a more advantageous position. When she finally fired her broadside, the *Fox* had no choice but to lower her flag and surrender. On their cruise home they fell in with a small British squadron consisting of the *Rainbow* and two smaller vessels, which recaptured the *Fox* and also captured the *Hancock* (Thurman 2016). Nevertheless, the damage was done. The British reputation at sea was sullied (Janzen 2013, 227). In 1779 another British naval vessel, the brig *Diligent,* was captured by the *Providence* of the Rhode Island navy off Newfoundland (Volo 2006, 52–53). Clearly, the Americans did not think the British were nearly as invulnerable at sea as the Empire would have had people believe.

American privateer activity was so bad that the migratory fishing trade to and from Newfoundland was destroyed. Even after the war, resident fishermen would have to make up much of the labor lost by the migratory trade (Rusted 2011, 16). Losses at sea were so bad that a group of Newfoundland merchants banded together in 1778 to appeal to the British government. If the government would send more ships to defend them against the American privateers, the merchants would defray the cost of coastal defenses. This could have been a costly endeavor for the merchants had the government sent the ships, but nothing seems to have come of it. Once again, the wheels of British bureaucracy turned too slowly to keep up with events (Bannister 2003, 163).

Perhaps the costliest naval loss for the British in financial terms occurred not to Newfoundland ships but in Newfoundland waters. In mid-July of 1779 a squadron of American ships, including the *Providence,* the *Queen of France* and the *Ranger*, came upon the homeward-bound Jamaica fleet in a dense fog off of Newfoundland. These ships were loaded with sugar and molasses and other goods produced in the Caribbean and bound for England. The Americans captured eleven of the ships and managed to get eight of them safely back to port, where their goods were sold to benefit the American cause (Fowler 1976, 101).

The Newfoundland squadron of the British Navy had their hands full with the American privateers that were constantly raiding the Newfoundland fishing grounds. Their problems did not get any easier as the war went on, for soon England's centuries-old foe would join forces with the rebelling American colonies.

Chapter 5

THE FRENCH JOIN THE FIGHT

The first indication in the Newfoundland fisheries that something was changing came in the fall of 1777. A French frigate came cruising into the Newfoundland fishing grounds with flags firing and signal guns blazing away every time a French fishing vessel was spotted. All the fishing vessels were ordered back to France regardless of how well or poorly loaded they were (J. Williams 1777). There would be no more French fishing in Newfoundland for five years.

The coming of 1778 changed the war in Newfoundland dramatically. Following the humiliating and costly defeats of the last two years, England decided to start spending more money on the defense of Newfoundland and of the fishery. The entrance of France into the war on the side of the Americans only sped this up.

French involvement in the war was the worst-kept secret of the American Revolution prior to 1778. St. Pierre and Miquelon, islands just south of Newfoundland, were ideally located to smuggle arms and other goods into the colonies. St. Pierre was one of the key ports in Pierre-Augustin Caron de Beaumarchais's plan to sell French goods to the colonies clandestinely. Better known by his nom-de-plum, Beaumarchais, Caron received loans from the French crown to a shell company which would buy surplus military items which would then be shipped to one of several ports, including St. Pierre in the western hemisphere. Once there, the weapons would be traded for American exports like tobacco, rice, wheat, or lumber, and brought into America via smuggling or some other ruse (Rupert 2017). St. Pierre was also a convenient spot for American privateers to put in for food, water, and rest while they attacked shipping on the Grand Banks. At least one American ship was spotted at St. Pierre when a British ship was forced to put into the harbor there by bad weather (O'Flaherty 1999, 99).

For these reasons, as soon as word was received that France and Britain were at war, Admiral John Montagu, who had been in charge of Newfoundland since 1776, moved in 1778 to quickly seize the two islands. His forces burned or destroyed every structure from house, to stage, to flake. They deported all the residents of the islands back to France (Prowse [1895] 2007, 340). Hearing about this destruction, the Comte d'Estaing wrote to George Washington, "we hope that with your assistance the day will come, when France shall partake in the Cod-fishery with other nations" (d'Estaing 1778). While they would not take the islands back by military force, the French did regain the islands by treaty at the end of the war.

The French Join the Fight

In the meantime, England did set about strengthening the defenses of Newfoundland. After the French and Indian War ended, the English started constructing or strengthening four fortifications in the city of St. John's: Fort William, which had originally been built in 1680 to fend off pirates; The Queen's Battery; Crow's Nest Battery on Gibbet Hill; and Fort Amherst and a chain that blocked the mouth of the harbor. These fortifications were completed and strengthened. A new battery was built at Quidi Vidi. Another was built at Cuckold's Cove (Rusted 2011, 31). The fortifications at Placentia were also strengthened (O'Neil 2003, 57–58). Robert Pringle, a military engineer who had been sent to Newfoundland in 1772, completed work on another fort, Fort Townshend, which would serve as the headquarters of the Newfoundland garrison from 1779 on. Pringle also built Military Road to connect Fort Townshend with Fort William and a road to Signal Hill (Fardy 1995, 37-38).

Pringle's next step was to raise manpower on the island to serve in his fortifications. Most of the soldiers stationed in Newfoundland since before the beginning of the war were old, sick, or otherwise infirm—the invalids of the army. They often lacked proper provisions and heating fuel, and they rarely received their proper clothing allowance (Kerr 1941). In 1779 Pringle was authorized to raise a three-hundred-man regiment to be known as His Majesty's Newfoundland Regiment of Foot. This regiment would have equipment and uniforms but would not be on the army's official list, nor would the recruits receive a bounty, as they would if they joined a regular army regiment.

Still, Pringle quickly filled his allotted ranks. He also raised another 350 men in a militia regiment to support his "regulars." The fear of an attack by the French inspired Newfoundland's men and boys to serve their King while staying as close to home as possible. There was also an abundance of men living on the island now. The war had caused a population boom on the island as fishermen chose to stay on the island rather than face an ocean crossing and the possibility of being captured by American ships. They also feared returning to English-controlled waters where they might be subject to impressment into the British navy, which would put them in harm's way aboard a man-of-war. His Majesty's Newfoundland Regiment of Foot was disbanded at the end of the war.

In 1778 the British ship *Proteus* sailed into St. John's and was found to be unseaworthy. She was hulked. Her rigging, sails, ropes, and masts were cannibalized by other ships on the station, desperate for supplies. The hull of the ship itself would serve as a prison for Americans captured by the Newfoundland squadron (Janzen 2013, 200). By 1780 her cannons had been spread out to several small outports to be used by their residents to defend themselves against the increasingly common practice of landing and raiding shore locations. St. Mary's, Trepassey, Harbour Grace, Fogo, Ferryland, Renews, Torbay, and Bay Bulls all received cannons.

The guns at St. Mary's are the most famous, as they

were used in September of 1782 to force the surrender of an American privateer, the *Hazzard*. The people of the town were granted prize money for the capture. This was a common naval practice of the time in which a ship's crew that captured another ship would receive money totaling the value of the ship and her cargo. Most shares of the prize money would go to the admiral who ultimately commanded the ship and the officers of the ship, but enough money went to the crew that they sometimes made more than their entire year's pay for capturing one ship. Paid in a lump sum, this often led to epic bouts of debauchery when the sailors were ashore. In this case the town's people also received the governor's usual share, which he conceded to the people because of their "spirited conduct" (Whiffen 2018).

Other places were not as lucky. During the summer of 1778 as many as twenty-two vessels were cut out of various harbors. Privateers would literally sneak into the harbors, generally in small boats, board the larger vessels, cut their anchor or mooring lines, and sail them away (O'Flaherty 1999, 100). American privateers attacked Sandwich Bay, Labrador in the summer of 1778 and captured £14,000 worth of goods and carried off thirty-six servants (Ryan 2012). In the spring of 1779 Twillingate was attacked by the *Centipede*. They took a vessel loaded with fish and attacked the house of a man named John Slade. Many of his possessions were distributed to the other people of Twillingate, which seems to indicate Slade may not have been a popular figure in the town (*Notre*

Dame Bay, Newfoundland and The American Revolution 2008). In many cases these attacks on outposts were very personal. The privateer captains who sailed their vessels into the harbors to plunder had often been merchant captains who, before the war, had sailed their ships into the same harbors to trade. (Prowse [1895] 2007).

A merchant by the name of Jeremiah Coughlan was largely responsible for the defense of Fogo Island. In 1778 his property in Chateau Bay, Labrador was attacked by privateers and he was bound and determined to prevent that from happening to his Fogo property. Coughlan raised a militia consisting of sixty-seven men. Governor Richard Edwards sent the cannon from the *Proteus* along with muskets to Coughlan and his militia. They were able to prevent any significant raids on Fogo for the duration of the war (Clarke 2016, 147, 226).

By 1780 the British were finally able to start sending enough ships to Newfoundland to combat American privateering and raiding. The British took or sank forty privateer ships that summer. Perhaps their most important capture was the packet vessel *Mercury* (captained by William Pickles) by the British frigate *Vestal*. When the *Vestal* came into view, Captain Pickles turned and ran, doing everything he could to escape the British frigate, but within five or six hours the *Vestal* caught up to him. Aboard the *Mercury* was Henry Laurens, a former president of the Continental Congress and recently appointed minister to the Netherlands. When it was apparent his ship was about to be taken, Laurens attempted to throw his diplomatic papers overboard as was his duty. Laurens cast out the paper in a bag weighted with iron shot in the hopes it would sink quickly, but "the weight proved insufficient for the purpose intended" (Laurens 1780). Unfortunately for Laurens, the *Vestal* had a rare asset aboard for a British man-of-war, a sailor who could swim. The sailor dove into the water and retrieved the package of papers (*New York Times*, "The Case of Mr. Laurens" 1801).

Figure 7. Henry Laurens. Courtesy of the Library of Congress.

Captain George Keppel of the *Vestal* took his prize into St. John's Harbor where the crew was no doubt put aboard the prison hulk *Proteus*. Laurens was kept on the *Vestal* for several weeks while Admiral Richard Edwards, who had taken over command of the Newfoundland squadron from Admiral Montagu, inspected the papers that had been found (*South Carolina Historical and Geneaological Magazine* 1905, 137–160). Among them he found evidence that convinced him a French invasion of Newfoundland was imminent. He also found a draft treaty between the United States and the Netherlands. (*New York Times* 1801).

Admiral Edwards quickly dispatched his valuable

prizes to London on the *Fairy*. Once there, Laurens was put in the Tower of London, where he would remain for fifteen months. The draft treaty that Laurens had been unable to destroy was used by the English as an excuse to declare war on the Dutch, in what became known as the Fourth Anglo-Dutch war, which was a complete disaster for the Dutch. Most notably, the British gained the right to trade in the Dutch East Indies, breaking the Dutch long- held monopoly and doing massive financial damage to the Netherlands.

Word of a massive French fleet assembling in 1781 in French ports soon reached Newfoundland. Many Newfoundlanders and the British military officers tasked with defending the island were sure that this was the invasion they had been preparing for. Soldiers were put on alert, muskets were obsessively cleaned, swords and bayonets were sharpened, and fortifications were checked and rechecked for weaknesses. Someone was always watching the horizon for the first sign of the topsails of the French fleet that would make their lives hell.

But the French fleet bypassed Newfoundland, instead sailing for the Chesapeake Bay. There they helped to close a trap on General Charles Cornwallis and his British army at the town of Yorktown. Cornwallis had begun his attack on the American South in 1779, taking the city of Charleston, South Carolina. Over the next year he pushed north in North Carolina in an attempt to bring the Southern American colonies back under British control. Although he met with some initial success, he

The French Join the Fight

Figure 8. "Surrender of Lord Cornwallis, at Yorktown, Virginia, October 19, 1781." Courtesy of the New York Public Library

found himself faced in 1781 by pieces of the army commanded by Marie-Joseph Paul Yves Roch Gilbert du Motier, Marquis de La Fayette—better known as simply the Marquis de Lafayette, a French national who had joined the Americans in 1777—and General Nathanael Greene, a Quaker from Rhode Island who had put aside his faith's pacifist ways to become one of the most solid tactical generals of the war. Cornwallis found himself retreating toward the coast and entrenched at the town of Yorktown, Virginia where he awaited reinforcement from the British commander in New York City, Sir Henry Clinton. Greene and Lafayette were soon joined by George Washington and a French army under the command of Jean Baptiste Donatien de Vimeur, comte de Rochambeau. The French fleet defeated the British fleet trying to relieve Yorktown at the Battle of the Chesapeake, and Cornwallis's fate was sealed. After a brief siege, and with no possibility of relief coming from the sea, Cornwallis surrendered.

While most of his soldiers were sent to prisoner-of-war camps, Cornwallis was exchanged by the Americans for the only high-value prisoner the British held, Henry Laurens. Once free, Laurens joined other American negotiators in Paris, including—Benjamin Franklin, John Jay, and eventually John Adams—in trying to end the war.

Yorktown was the final major battle of the war between the Americans and the British, yet even as fighting in America slowly died down following the Battle of Yorktown, the battle for Newfoundland was still raging. This time it would be a war of words. The negotiations between Great Britain and the young United States would be a fight for the cod.

Chapter 6

THE WAR OF WORDS

The value that the New England colonies and later states put on the Newfoundland fishery cannot be understated. They were fully aware of the financial value of the trade in fish, as seen in earlier chapters. They were also acutely aware that they had shed blood right alongside British soldiers to secure Newfoundland's fishing grounds for the British Empire. Americans had been among the troops at Louisburg in 1758 and at Signal Hill in 1762. They had fought the elements to fish for cod for years. They felt as entitled to fish the grounds as anyone else in the British world even if they were actively attempting to separate themselves from it.

Historian Christopher P. Magra (2004, 561) put it as simply as possible when he said the "Northern contingent of Congress would not settle for peace without fishing rights." Thomas Cushing , who was then the Lieutenant Governor of Massachusetts, said nearly the same thing in 1781: "England must now think seriously of negotiating, which I pray God may issue in a beneficial, Permeant and Honorable Peace, however I am confident it will not be thought so by the Northern States unless their share of the Fishery upon the banks of Newfoundland are secured to them" (1781).

On September 20, 1778 John Adams had written to Ralph Izard, who was then serving as the American Commissioner to the Court of Tuscany, that he (Adams) was apprehensive about negotiating for the right to fish the Banks of Newfoundland. He was afraid it would become the subject of controversy and maybe the cause of more war with Britain, or even France (Adams 1778). This was a commonly held belief, especially among those who doubted France's true intentions in allying itself with the rebelling colonies in the war. In 1779 James Lovell, a delegate for Massachusetts to the Continental Congress, wrote to Adams, "France to be sure would never think, at least would never insist that a common Right in the fishery was included in our independence" (Lovell 1779).

Izard responded to Adams's letter of September 20 four days later with a logical response that put Adams's mind at ease. He pointed out that the fisheries of Holland were a major factor in their rise as a republic and argued: "The fishery of Newfoundland appears to me to be a mine of infinitely greater value than Mexico and Peru. It enriches the proprietors, is worked at less expense and is the source of naval strength and protection" (Izard 1778). From then on, John Adams seemed to understand the importance of the fishery, although it was often a point of contention between the English and the Americans.

Peace negotiations between the United States and

The War of Words

Great Britain began in earnest in early 1782. After peace and independence for the former colonies, rights to the fisheries were among the most important and most haggled-over points in the entire negotiations. The debate over fish lasted for months. John Adams wrote to Richard Cranch, a Boston-area merchant and his brother-in-law, "Since my Arrival here 26 October until the 30 November, We had a constant scuffle Morning, noon and night about cod and Haddock on the Grand Banks" (15 December 1782). Robert R. Livingston, American Secretary of Foreign Affairs, had warned another of the chief negotiators of the peace treaty, Benjamin Franklin, of just such a possibility in early 1782. He wrote, "The fisheries will probably be another source of Litigation, not because our rights are doubtful, but because Great Britain has never paid much attention to rights which interfere with her Views" (7 January 1782). In other words the fisheries would be contested not over any other question of whether American fishermen had the right to be there but because the British would be unwilling to share the grounds. In August he reminded Franklin again: "the fisheries are too important an object for you to lost site [*sic*] of" (9 August 1782).

Of course, by the time Franklin finally received this letter, thanks to the slow travel of mail in the eighteenth century, negotiations over the fishery were nearly over. Franklin (1782) replied to Livingston in October with an explanation of what they had negotiated for thus far. "By another article the fisheries in American Seas is to be freely exercised by the Americans wherever they might formerly exercise it while united with Great Britain." In December, John Adams wrote a celebratory letter to his friend Elbridge Gerry, a former Continental Congressman from Massachusetts, about the end of negotiations for fish. "Thanks be to God, my dear Gerry, that our Tom Cod are Safe, in spite of the Malice of Enemies the finesse of Allies and the Mistakes of Congress" (14 December 1782). In a more melancholy mood the following month, Adams (1783) wrote to his wife Abigail, "My children will have nothing but their Liberty and the Right to Catch Fish on the Banks of Newfoundland. This is all the Fortune that I have been able to make for myself or them."

Figure 9. John Adams. Courtesy of the Library of Congress.

No matter how Adams felt about the treaty, up or down, the definitive treaty with England was signed on September 30, 1783. In the first article of the treaty Great Britain acknowledged the independence of the United States. In the second, boundaries for the new country were established. The third article of the treaty gave Americans the right to fish the Grand Banks. They were only restricted from drying their catch on Newfoundland, which they would now have to do in Labrador or Nova Scotia. It is not until article seven of the treaty that the negotiators got around to declaring peace between the two countries. In the treaty, the fishery is given more importance than peace.

That seems like such a nice simple ending, but diplomacy very rarely wraps up neatly with a bow. The United States had negotiated its peace treaty with Great Britain separately and in relative secrecy from the French, their chief allies during the war. The Americans had dangled many ideas about Newfoundland to France during the war, both before and after their alliance was official. In 1776 William Hooper, Congressional delegate from North Carolina wrote, "We have been holding forth new lines to France, by offering what we have not to give & provided they will conquer the whole of Newfoundland & secure the fishing, that we will most bountifully & most graciously give them one half of it for their trouble" (*Letters of the Delegates to Congress* 1979, 688). The Franco-American Treaty of Amity and Commerce from 1778 guaranteed that the Americans would not interfere with French fishing on the Banks of Newfoundland or on the French Shore established by the Treaty of Utrecht. But as early of 1777 the Americans had offered the idea of France and the United States taking over Newfoundland and sharing the fishery exclusively between the two of them (Gerry 1777). France had actually recalled her fishing fleet from Newfoundland in 1777 (J. Williams 1777). The following year they did not even send out a fishing fleet—the sailors instead being pressed to man the French war fleet ("Intelligence from Brest, 12 January 1778" 1778). In 1779 Benjamin Franklin had again broached the idea or a conjoined attack on Newfoundland by the two countries following a fire in St. John's that destroyed a good deal of the town's military supplies (Franklin 1779).

The Americans did not want France to completely take over Newfoundland for themselves though. One of the major opponents of this idea was George Washington, who wrote to Henry Laurens in 1778 that the French should be discouraged from attacking Canada as it could lead to them "engrossing the whole trade of Newfoundland whenever she pleased." Not only was Washington against losing the trade but he was also against losing "the finest nursery of seamen in the world" (Washington 1778).

Of course, France had her own interests to look after. They realized that the Americans would be another competitor in the cod fish market if they won the right to the fishery. To them this was not ideal. In 1781 the British captured a letter from François Barbé-Marbois, Secretary of the French legation to the United States, to Charles

Gravier, comte de Vergennes, the French Minister of Foreign Affairs—which said bluntly the Americans had no right to the fishery. They let the letter slip to the Americans (Dangerfield 1960, 165). This may have played a role in the American peace commissioners' willingness to negotiate without the French in their corner. In 1782 John Adams (18 November 1782) wrote to Robert R. Livingston about his advice to counsel with the French during the negotiations: "If we are counselled to relinquish our right to the fishery on the Grand Banks of Newfoundland, when the British Ministry are ready by Treaty to acknowledge our Right to it, are we obliged to relinquish it?" Clearly, Adams was beyond trusting the French in the negotiations.

The French and the English did in fact strike a separate peace. Ironically, because of the quicker travel between the two countries than between Europe and the United States, the peace between Britain and France was actually signed first—on September 3, 1783. In this treaty England retained full ownership of Newfoundland but did return St. Pierre and Miquelon to the French. The British had briefly considered giving the French Fogo instead of St. Pierre and Miquelon, but Jeremiah Coughlan had showed how easy it was to defend Fogo with a few men, and that ran counter to British interests. The treaty also moved the French Shore of Newfoundland from the northern shore to western shore, between Cape St. John and Cape Ray. The main reason for moving the French Shore was to avoid uprooting the English who had settled there in the absence of the French. The French were also allowed to keep a piece of the fishery to avoid the embarrassment of having their ally, the United States, join the British in the fishery while they were excluded. This kind of loss of face could easily have led to another war (Thompson 1961, 15).

The Dutch decided that, despite the fact they had only recognized the United States as a county in 1782 but had never formed an alliance with the new nation and were losing quite soundly to the English in the Fourth Anglo-Dutch War, they should expect some part of the American fishery. On April 25, 1780 William Lee wrote to John Adams, "The Dutch who are so jealous of any other nation but themselves catching a herring on the open sea, think it not unreasonable or immodest to expect exclusive privileges in some part of the American trade and an equal Freedom with others, to the fishery on the banks of Newfoundland" (Lee 1780). The fishery had been virtually an exclusive right of the English and the French for the entirety of the seventeenth century, with the English being able to set the terms upon which the French fished—so this belief by the Dutch that they could suddenly rejoin the trade was amusing at best. Adams responded four days later (29 April 1780): "The Dutch may expect what they please, but they will expect for Eternity, if they expect one Iota of an exclusive privilege in American Trade. I wonder in God's name what obligation we are under to the Dutch? Nor can I conceive what pretensions they can have to the fishery, on the

The War of Words

Banks of Newfoundland." Eventually, the Dutch signed their own Treaty of Paris with England with no fishing concessions from them or the Americans.

With the signing of the treaties, peace once again returned to Newfoundland and the world. Fishing vessels from the newly independent United States, England, and France could once again ply their trade on the Grand Banks. Hundreds of ships set out to fish in the next season hoping to regain a sense of normalcy. On those ships were thousands of boys on their first fishing voyages. They would have to quickly learn the skills of the fishery so that in a season or two they could become the seasoned hands that would pass on their knowledge to the next generation. As Jean-François Briere observed, the war "did not stop the training of sailors but did stop training of codfishermen" (Briere 1992, 203).

Figure 10. The French Shore: 1783 through 1904. Courtesy of Newfoundland and Labrador Heritage (Hiller 2001).

EPILOGUE

With the signing of the peace treaties that ended the American Revolution, harmony returned to Newfoundland and her fishing grounds—at least as much as the temperamental North Atlantic Ocean allowed. There was a sense of a return to the status quo. Once again, the French and English shared the island uneasily. Fleets of ships from France, England, and the newly independent United States began to work the waters of the Grand Banks again, seeking to restore the supply of fish to the Caribbean and Southern Europe that had been disrupted by the war.

Americans were no longer welcome to set foot on the island. They were forced to dry their cod elsewhere, and they certainly were not allowed to bring food and other provisions to the island to trade, although some small-scale trading between the captains of individual vessels kept a small flow of American goods going to Newfoundland. That arrangement lasted all of three years, until 1786, when a food shortage forced the British to allow trading with the Americans again (Ryan 2012,

157). None of this replaced the income from the trade in fish with the Caribbean which had been cut off during the war and not reestablished after it. It is estimated that, on Jamaica alone, some fifteen thousand enslaved people starved to death because of the lack of trade (Kurlansky 1998, 100).

Figure 11. An American Brig in Trepassey Harbour,, 1786 Courtesy of Newfoundland and Labrador Heritage. (Butt 1998)

On the island, though, the status quo had been forever changed. The former fishermen and women who stayed on the island rather than face the dangers of a wartime Atlantic crossing had forged a new way of life for themselves (Cadigan 1995, 24). They had become farmers, loggers and artisans—and even seal hunters, since seal blubber could be rendered into oil to replace the whale oil they were no longer getting from New England (Major 2002, 295). They built truly permanent settlements on Newfoundland. They had families. The population grew

Epilogue

from five thousand in 1765 to at least ten thousand by the mid-1780s (Newfoundland Historical Society 2008, 55). A decade later, the outbreak of the French Revolution and the subsequent Napoleonic Wars only reinforced this population growth, as the renewed wars in Europe exposed the fisherman to the same dangers they had faced during the American Revolution. It was safer to stay in Newfoundland than to cross the Atlantic and risk capture or death at the hands of the French, or impressment by the British navy (Hancock 2003, 137). The monopoly of the West Country merchants had been broken and they would now have to deal with the population on the island as true subjects of the British crown and not as wild men living on the fringes of civilization (Campey 2016, 56).

The British government changed its view of Newfoundland as well. Newfoundland would never have the same rights that the former colonies in America once had. The English government tightened their control of the island, fearing a centralization of power that could lead to rebellion like that in the former colonies (Cadigan 1995, 29). Now that the King and Parliament had almost complete control of the island, they certainly were not going to risk losing it to another rebellion.

During the American Revolution, Newfoundland had found itself a target, a fort, a source of soldiers and sailors, and a bone of contention among peace negotiators. After the war though, Newfoundland found itself to be something entirely different. No longer was it a simple fishing station. Newfoundland was a real place where real people lived and were beginning to develop a sense of identity of what it would mean to be a Newfoundlander—hardy people who could thrive in whatever the world threw at them, be it manmade fiascos or nature's fury.

BIBLIOGRAPHY

Adams, John. 1782. "From John Adams to Elbridge Gerry, 14 December 1782." *Founders Online*/National Archives–National Historical Publications and Records Commission (NA–NHPRC). December 14. Accessed September 27, 2019. https://founders.archives.gov/documents/Adams/06-14-02-0074.

—. 1778. "From John Adams to Ralph Izard, 20 September 1778." *Founders Online*/NA–NHPRC. September 20. Accessed September 27, 2017. https://founders.archives.gov/documents/Adams/06-07-02-0042.

—. 1782. "From John Adams to Robert R. Livingston, 18 November 1782." *Founders Online*/NA–NHPRC. November 18. Accessed September 27, 2019. https://founders.archives.gov/documents/Adams/06-14-02-0035.

—. 1780. "From John Adams to William Lee, 29 April 1780." *Founders Online*/NA–NHPRC. April 29. Accessed January 5, 2020. https://founders.archives.gov/documents/Adams/06-09-02-0142.

—. 1783. "John Adams to Abigail Adams, 22 January 1783." *Founders Online*/NA–NHPRC. January 22. Accessed September 27, 2019. https://founders.archives.gov/documents/Adams/04-05-02-0040.

—. 1775. "John Adams to Isaac Smith Sr., 7 June 1775."

Founders Online/NA–NHPRC. June 7. Accessed October 6, 2019. https://founders.archives.gov/documents/Adams/04-01-02-0143.

—. 1782. "John Adams to Richard Cranch, 15 December 1782." *Founders Online*/NA–NHPRC. December 15. Accessed September 27, 2019. https://founders.archives.gov/documents/Adams/04-05-02-0026.

Banks, Joseph. 1971. *Joseph Banks in Newfoundland and Labroador, 1766, His Diary, Manuscripts and Collections.* Edited by A. M. Lysaght. Berkley: University Of California Press.

Bannister, Jerry. 1998. "Convict Transport and the Colonial State in Newfoundland, 1789." *Acadiensis* 27 (2).

—. 2003. *The Rule of The Admirals: Law, Custom and Naval Government in Newfoundland, 1699-1832.* Toronto: University of Toronto Press.

Briere, Jean-François. 1992. "The French Codfishing Industry in North America and the Crisis of the Pre-Revolutionary Years, 1783-1792." *Proceedings of the Meeting of the French Colonial Historical Society*, 201-210.

Brutiere, G. Anquetil. 1778. "To Benjamin Franklin from G. Anquetil Brutiere, 7 June 1778: résumé." *Founders Online*/NA–NHPRC. June 7. Accessed September 27, 2019. https://founders.archives.gov/documents/Franklin/01-26-02-0534.

Butt, Jeff. 1998. "Labrador Fishery." *Heritage Newfoundland and Labrador.* Accessed October 17, 2019. https://www.heritage.nf.ca/articles/exploration/labrador-fishery.php.

Cadigan, Sean T. 1995. *Hope and Deception in Conception Bay: Merchant-Settler Relations in Newfoundland, 1785-1855.* Toronto: University of Toronto Press.

Campey, Lucille H. 2016. *Atlantic Canada's Irish Immigrants: A Fish and Timber Story.* Toronto: Dundurn.

Clarke, David J. 2016. *A History of the Isles.* Self Published.

Bibliography

Cushing, Thomas. 1781. "To Benjamin Franklin from Thomas Cushing, 26 October 1781." *Founders Online*/NA–NHPRC. October 26. Accessed September 27, 2019. https://founders.archives.gov/documents/Franklin/01-35-02-0498.

Dangerfield, George. 1960. *Chancellor Robert R. Livingston of New York, 1746-1813.* Harcourt Brace and Company.

d'Estaing. 1778. "To George Washington from Vice Admiral d'Estaing, 6 October 1778." *Founders Online*/NA–NHPRC. October 6. Accessed September 27, 2019. https://founders.archives.gov/documents/Washington/03-17-02-0295.

European Migratory Fishery/*Heritage Newfoundland and Labrador. 1997.* Accessed October 14, 2019. https://www.heritage.nf.ca/articles/exploration/european-migratory-fishery.php.

Fardy, Bernard D. 1995. *Before Beaumont Hamel: The Newfoundland Regiment 1775-1815.* St. John's: Creative Publishers.

Fitzgerald, John. 1777. "To George Washington from Colonel John Fitzgerald, 19 February 1777." *Founders Online*/NA–NHPRC. February 19. Accessed September 27, 2019. https:/founders.archives.gov/documents/Washington/03-08-02-0402.

Fowler, William M. 1976. *Rebels Under Sail: The American Nevy During the Revolution.* New York: Charles Scribner's Sons.

Franklin, Benjamin. 1767. "Right, Wrong, and Reasonable, 18 April 1767." *Founders Online*/NA–NHPRC. April 18. Accessed January 7, 2020. https://founders.archives.gov/documents/Franklin/01-14-02-0068.

—. 1782. "From Benjamin Franklin to Robert R. Livingston, 14 October 1782." *Founders Online*/NA–NHPRC. October 14. Accessed September 27, 2019. https://founders.archives.gov/documents/Franklin/01-38-02-0165.

—. 1779. "From Benjamin Franklin to Sartine, 22 October 1779." *Founders Online*/NA–NHPRC. October 22. Accessed September 22, 2019. https://founders.archives.gov/documents/Franklin/01-30-02-0456.

—. 1775. "Proposed Memorial to Lord Dartmouth, 16 March 1775." *Founders Online*/NA–NHPRC. March 16. Accessed January 1, 2020. https://founders.archives.gov/documents/Franklin/01-21-02-0294.

—. 1729. "The Busy-Body, No. 8, 27 March 1729." *Founders Online*/NA–NHPRC. March 27. Accessed September 27, 2019. https://founders.archives.gov/documents/Franklin/01-01-02-0040.

Gerry, Elbridge. 1777. "To John Adams from Elbridge Gerry, 8 January 1777." *Founders Online*/NA–NHPRC. January 8. Accessed September 27, 2019. https://founders.archives.gov/documents/Adams/06-05-02-0035.

Gordon, William. 1777. "To George Washington from William Gordon, 17 July 1777." *Founders Online*/NA–NHPRC. July 17. Accessed September 27, 2019. https://founders.archives.gov/documents/Washington/03-10-02-0301.

Hancock, W. Gordon. 2003. *"Soe longe as there comes noe women": Origins of English Settlement in Newfoundland.* Milton: Global Heritage Presss Inc.

Hiller, J. K. 2001. "The French Treaty Shore." *Heritage Newfoundland and Labrador.* Accessed October 14, 2019. https://www.heritage.nf.ca/articles/exploration/french-shore.php.

Horwood, Harold. 2011. *Plunder and Pillage: Atlantic Canada's Brutal and Bloodthirsty Pirates and Privateers.* Halifax: Formac Publishing Company.

"Intelligence from Brest, 12 January 1778." 1778. *Founders Online*/NA–NHPRC. January 12. Accessed September

27, 2019. https://founders.archives.gov/documents/Franklin/01-25-02-0369.

Izard, Ralph. 1778. "To John Adams from Ralph Izard, 24 September 1778." *Founders Online*/NA–NHPRC. September 24. Accessed September 27, 2019. https://founders.archives.gov/documents/Adams/06-07-02-0051.

Janzen, Olaf. 2001. "The Revolution as Opportunity." *Heritage Newfoundland and Labrador.* Accessed October 20, 2019. https://www.heritage.nf.ca/articles/exploration/revolution-opportunity.php .

Janzen, Olaf U. 2013. *War and Trade in Eighteenth Century Newfoundland.* St. John's: International Maritime Economic History Association.

Janzen, Olaf Uwe. 2001. "The Restoration to France (1763-1815)." *Heritage Newfoundland and Labrador.* Accessed October 14, 2019. https://www.heritage.nf.ca/articles/exploration/restoration-france.php.

Kerr, W. B. 1941. "Newfoundland in the Period Before the American Revolution." *The Pennsylvania Magazine of History and Biography*, January: 56-78.

Kurlansky, Mark. 1998. *Cod: A Biography of the Fish That Changed the World.* New York: Penguin Books.

Laurens, Henry. 1780. "Letter to the Committee on Foreign Affairs, Philadelphia." *The New York Public Library.* September 14. Accessed January 8, 2020. https://digitalcollections.nypl.org/items/bac0a75c-258a-b981-e040-e00a18067fd9.

Lee, William. 1780. "To John Adams from William Lee, 25 April 1780." *Founders Online*/NA–NHPRC. April 25. Accessed January 4, 2020. https://founders.archives.gov/documents/Adams/06-09-02-0131.

Letters of Delegates to Congress 1774-1789. 1976. Vol. 1. Washington, DC: Library of Congress.

Letters of the Delegates of Congress, 1774-1789. 1979. Vol. 5. Washington, DC: Library of Congress.

Livingston, Robert R. 1783. "To Benjamin Franklin from Robert R. Livingston, 6 January 1783." *Founders Online.* January 6. Accessed January 6, 2020. https://founders.archives.gov/documents/Franklin/01-38-02-0418.

—. 1782. "To Benjamin Franklin from Robert R. Livingston, 7 January 1782." *Founders Online*/NA–NHPRC. January 7. Accessed September 27, 2019. https://founders.archives.gov/documents/Franklin/01-36-02-0267.

—. 1782. "To Benjamin Franklin from Robert R. Livingston, 9 August 1782." *Founders Online*/NA–NHPRC. August 9. Accessed September 27, 2019. https://founders.archives.gov/documents/Franklin/01-37-02-0475.

Lords of the Admiralty, The. 1779. "Letter to Nicholas Vincent, senior captain at Plymouth." *New York Public Library.* January 25. Accessed January 3, 2020. https://digitalcollections.nypl.org/items/bac0a75c-27aa-b981-e040-e00a18067fd9.

Lovell, James. 1779. "To John Adams from James Lovell, 1 November 1779." *Founders Online*/NA–NHPRC. November 1. Accessed September 27, 2019. https://founders.archives.gov/documents/Adams/06-08-02-0163.

Magra, Christopher P. 2004. "'Soldiers...Bred to the Sea': Maritime Marblehead, Massachusetts, and the Origins and Progress of the American Revolution." *The New England Quarterly* 77 (4): 531–562.

—. 2007. "The New England Cod Fishing Industry and Maritime Dimensions of the American Revolution." *Enterprise and Society*, December: 799–806.

Magra, Christopher Paul. 2007. "Beyond the Banks: The Integrated Wooden Working World of Eighteenth-Century Massachusetts' Codfisheries." *The Northern Mariner* XVII: 1-16.

Bibliography

—. 2006. "The New Egland Cod Fishing Industry and Maritime Dimensions of the American Revolution."

Major, Kevin. 2002. *As Near to Heaven By Sea: A History of Newfoundland and Labrador.* Toronto: Penguin.

Matthews, Keith. 1988. *Lectures on the History of Newfoundland, 1500-1830.* St. John's : Breakwater Books.

Morris, Richard B. 1965. *The Peacemakers: The Great Powers and American Independence.* New York: Harper & Row.

New York Gazette. 1775. April 24.

New York Journal. 1775. "Extract of a letter from Newfoundland Dated June 12." August 24: 3.

New York Times. 1801. "The Case of Mr. Laurens." November 23.

Newfoundland Historical Society. 2008. *A Short History of Newfoundland and Labrador.* Portugal Cove: Boulder Publications.

Notre Dame Bay, Newfoundland and The American Revolution. 2008. January 13. Accessed September 26, 2019. http://www.historica.ca/notre-dame-bay-newfoundland-and-the-american-revolution.php.

O'Flaherty, Patrick. 1999. *Old Newfoundland: A History to 1843.* St. John's: Long Beach Press.

O'Neil, Paul. 2003. *The Oldest City: The Story of St. John's, Newfoundland.* St. John's : Boulder Publications.

Palmer, Joseph. 1775. "To John Adams from Joseph Palmer, 2 December 1775." *Founders Online*/NA–NHPRC. December 2. Accessed September 27, 2019. https://founders.archives.gov/documents/Adams/06-03-02-0175.

Prowse, D. W. Originally published 1895, Republished 2007. *A History of Newfoundland.* Portugal Cove: Boulder Publications.

Rupert, Bob. 2017. "America's First Black Ops." *The Journal of the American Revolution.* September 5. Accessed

October 22, 2019. https://allthingsliberty.com/2017/09/americas-first-black-ops/.

Rusted, Joan. 2011. *St. John's: A Brief History.* St. John's: Breakwater Books.

Ryan, Shannon. 2012. *A History of Newfoundland in the North Atlantic to 1818.* St. John's: Flanker Press.

South Carolina Historical and Geneaological Magazine/South Carolina Historical Society. 1905. "Correspondence between Hon. Henry Laurens and his son John." October: 137–160.

Suthern, Victor. 2000. *To Go Upon Discovery: James Cook and Canada From 1758 to 1779.* Toronto: Dundurn Press.

—. 2000. *To Go Upon Discovery: James Cook and Canada from 1758-1779.* Toronto: Dundurn Press.

Thompson, Frederic F. 1961. *The French Shore Problem in Newfoundland: An Imperial Study.* Toronto: University of Toronto Press.

Thurman, Joel W. 2016. "The Revolution as Told by One of the Navy's Greatest Ships." *The Journal of the American Revolution.* November 16. Accessed October 22, 2019. https://allthingsliberty.com/2016/11/revolution-told-one-navys-greatest-ships/.

Tufts, Cotton. 1776. "Cotton Tufts to John Adams, 6 August 1776." *Founders Online*/NA–NHPRC. August 6. Accessed January 4, 2020. https://founders.archives.gov/documents/Adams/04-02-02-0050.

Volo, James M. 2006. *Blue Water Patriots: The American Revolution Afloat.* London: Rownan and Littlefield Publishers Inc.

Ward, Artemas. 1776. "To George Washington from Major General Artemas Ward, 14 November 1776." *Founders Online*/NA–NHPRC. November 14. Accessed September

27, 2019. https://founders.archives.gov/documents/Washington/03-07-02-0114.

Warren, James. 1775. "To John Adams from James Warren, 3 December 1775." *Founders Online*/NA–NHPRC. December 3. Accessed September 27, 2019. https://founders.archives.gov/documents/Adams/06-03-02-0179.

—. 1775. "To John Adams from James Warren, 31 July 1775." *Founders Online*/NA–NHPRC. July 31. Accessed September 27, 2019. https://founders.archives.gov/documents/Adams/06-03-02-0063.

Washington, George. 1778. "From George Washington to Henry Laurens, 14 November 1778." *Founders Online*/NA–NHPRC. November 14. Accessed September 27, 2019. https://founders.archives.gov/documents/Washington/03-18-02-0147.

Webb, Jeff. 2015. "William Knox and the 18th-Century Newfoundland Fishery." *Acadiensis* 44 (1): 112-122.

Whiffen, Glen. 2018. "Restoration of 1779 gun battery has St. Mary's charged." *The Telegram.* May 2. Accessed Sepember 24, 2019. https://www.thetelegram.com/news/local/restoration-of-1779-gun-battery-has-st-marys-charged-207065/.

Williams, Jonathan. 1777. *Founders Online*/NA–NHPRC. November 4.

Williams, Tony. 2009. *Hurricane of Independence: The Untold Story of the Deadly Storm at the Deciding Moment of the American Revolution.* Naperville: Source Books Inc.

INDEX

Adams,
   Abigail, 52
   John, 48, 50, 51, 52, 55
American Revolution, ix, x, xi, xii, 6, 23, 25, 59, 61
Amherst, William, 3
Arnold, Benedict, 29
artificers, 30
Avalon Peninsula, x, 4
Banks, Joseph, 8
Barbé-Marbois, François, 54
Bay Bulls, 36, 42
Beaumarchais, 40
Bellona, 36
Boston, 23, 35, 37, 51
Boston Port Act, 15, 16
Boston Tea Party, 15, 16
bread, 25
Brutiere, G. Anquetil, 36
Cahill, John, 9
Cape Bonavista, 2
Cape Race, 31
Cape Ray, 55

Cape St. John, 55
Caribbean, 38, 59, 60
Carleton, Guy, 28, 30
carpenters, 28
Castle Hill, x
Centipede, 43
Charles II, 1
Charleston, South Carolina, 46
Chesapeake Bay, 46
Clinton, Henry, 47
cod, xii, 23, 24, 35, 37, 48, 51, 54, 59
Cod,
Comte d'Estaing, 40
Comte d'Haussonville, 3
Comte deVergennes, 55
Conception Bay, 17, 19
Concord, 18
Continental Congress, 50
Cook, James, xi, 4
Cornwallis, Charles, 46, 47, 48

Index

Coughlan, Jeremiah, 44, 55
Cranch, Richard, 51
Cuckold's Cove, 41
Cushing, Thomas, 49
Dalton, Lawrence, 9
Declaration of Independence, xiii, 33, 34
Denmark, 1
Diligent, 37
East India Company, 15
Edwards, Richard, 44, 45
84th Regiment of Foot., 31
enslaved, 60
Fairy, 46
Ferryland, 42
Fogo, 42, 44, 55
Fort Amherst, 41
Fort Townshend, 41
Fort William, 3
42nd Regiment of Foot, 27, 28, 30
Fox, x, xi, 37
Fox Harbour, x, xi
France, ix, 36, 38, 50, 53, 54, 55, 57, 59
Franco-American Treaty of Amity and Commerce, 53
Franklin, Benjamin, 35, 36, 48, 51, 54
French and Indian War, 3, 27, 28, 41
French Revolution, 61

French Shore, 4, 6
Gerry, Elbridge, 52
Glover, John, 24
Grand Banks, 22, 37, 51, 53, 55, 57, 59
Great Britain, 21, 33, 34, 48, 51, 52, 53
Greene, Nathanael, 47
Hallohan, Lawrence, 9
Hancock, 35, 37
Harbour Grace, 42
Hazzard, 43
Holy Roman Empire, 1
Hooper, William, 53
Hopkins, Esek, 34
Howe, William, 24
Hungary, 1
hurricane, 13, 14, 19, 20
Ireland, 9, 21
Izard, Ralph, 50
Jamaica, 38, 60
Jay, John, 48
Jones, John Paul, 35
Keppel, George, 45
King's Orange Rangers, 32
Knox, William, 7
Labrador, 53
Lafayette, Marquis de, 47
Laurens, Henry, 48, 54
Lee, William, 56
Lexington, 18
Livingston, James, 28

73

Robert R., 51, 55
Long Island, 23
Lord North, 21
Louisburg, 49
Lovell, James, 50
Maclean, Colonel Allan, 31
Marblehead, 23
Massachusetts, 23, 35, 49, 50, 52
Melville, Elizabeth, 6
Mercury, 44
Mexico, 50
militia, 3, 31
molasses, 38
Montagu, John, 40, 45
Montgomery, Richard, 27, 28, 29
Moore, Ann, 6
Morgan, Daniel, 29, 30
Napoleonic Wars, 61
Netherlands, 1, 44, 45, 46
New Netherland, 13
New York, x, 23, 30, 32, 35
Newcastle Jane, 31
Newfoundland Regiment, 41, 42
Newfoundland Squadron, 7
Nova Scotia, 53
Ohio, 3
Palliser, Hugh, 21
Palliser's Act, 21
Palmer, Joseph, 20
Penguin, 36

Peru, 50
Pickles, William, 44
Placentia, x, 7, 32
Point Riche, 2
Portugal, 1, 11
Power, Richard, 9
Pringle, Robert, 41, 42
privateer, 31, 35, 36
Proteus, 42, 44, 45
Providence, 37, 38
Prussia, 1
Quebec, 30, 31
Quidi Vidi, 41
Ranger, 38
Rattlesnake, 35
Renews, 42
Rhode Island, 37
Rochambeau, Jean Baptiste Doantien de Vimeur de, 47
Romney, 34
rum, 8, 25
Saint Pierre and Miquelon, 4
Sandwich Bay, 43
Sardinia, 1
Savoy, 1
Schuyler, Philip, 28
Seven Years' War, 3
Shivers, Thomas Revelle, 36
Signal Hill, x, xiii, 3, 49
Smith, Sr., Isaac, 18
Spain, 1, 11
St. John's, x, xiii, 3, 7, 33, 54

Index

St. Mary's, 42
St. Pierre and Miquelon, 55
sugar, 38
Surprize, 34
Tea Act of 1773, 15
Torbay, 42
Tower of London, 46
Treaty of Utrecht, 4, 6, 54
Trenton, 24
Trepassey, 42
Trinity Bay, 19
Tufts, Cotton, 5
Twillingate, 43
Vestal, 44, 45
Virginia, 3, 47
Ward, Artemas, 35
Warren, James, 19, 20
Washington, George, 23, 35, 54
women, 4, 5, 8, 60
Yorktown, 48

ACKNOWLEDGMENTS

First and foremost, I need to thank my family—my wife Ashley and my children Katherine and James. Thank you for giving me the time to write this and for putting up with my in-depth discussions of my new discoveries over the dinner table—and also for picking up most of the books I used as sources from the post office. Thank you to my historian friends and even some of my non-historian friends who have listened to me talk out a great deal of this book before I ever set to typing. And thank you as well to the select few who read and reviewed for me—and to my parents, James and Linda, who brought me to Newfoundland and to the historic sites there—and to my Newfoundland family who have kept me feeling connected to that part of my family history.

I also owe a debt of gratitude to many of the libraries in the area where I live. Thank you for providing a quiet, comfortable place where I could sit and write.

And to Ashley, Kjirsten, and Dad—who read early versions of this and gave me their notes and thoughts without telling me to scrap the whole project—thanks so much.

ABOUT THE AUTHOR

Geoff Benton is a historian living in upstate New York with his wife and two kids in the only house in his neighborhood flying the Republic of Newfoundland flag. He is employed at a historic site by the New York State Office of Parks, Recreation and Historic Preservation. He received his BA in history and biology from the State University of New York at Potsdam and his MA in American History from the State University of New York at Albany. He has been actively employed in the history and historic preservation field for the last thirteen years.

He was the author of one previous book, *Kinderhook Reformed Church: 300 Years of Faith and Community*. You can find more of Geoff's writing at:
www.thechancellorscourt.blogspot.com

www.ingramcontent.com/pod-product-compliance
Lightning Source LLC
Chambersburg PA
CBHW030004050426
42451CB00006B/106